AMERICANA

POEMS FROM RICH MURPHY

AMERICANA

POEMS FROM RICH MURPHY

THE POETRY PRESS
Hollywood   Los Angeles

Published by
The Poetry Press of Press Americana
the press of

Americana:
The Institute for the Study of
American Popular Culture

http://www.americanpopularculture.com

Library of Congress Cataloging-in-Publication Data

Murphy, Richard, 1950-
[Poems. Selections]
Americana : Poems from Rich Murphy / [Rich Murphy].
pages cm
ISBN 978-0-9829558-7-1
I. Title.
PR6063.U735A6 2014
821'.914--dc23
                                2013040068

TABLE OF CONTENTS

City Slicker   1

Western State Penitentiary   1
Anthem   3
Viva Viva   4
New Species   5
Exterior Wash   6
The Bomb   7
The Service Station's Island   8
Par for the Course   9
Bear Right and Keep to the Left   10
The Pin Up Girls   11
American Gothic, Circa 1950, by Rote   12
American Dream   13
American Dream Extended   14
From Valley to Valet   15
Historical Data   16
The Head of Man   17
Orbital Dating Game   18

Lawn Art   19

Brush with Exposure   19
The Blotter   21
Movers   22
Pedestrian Poets   23
Courtship   24
Monument Boulevard Vacation   25
The Twain Shall Meet   26
Sounding From St Petersburg, Missouri   27
Portal Properties   28
Now, The Fashion Celebrity   29
That's Precision   30

Hot House Homes   32
Neither Rhyme nor Season   33
Capital's Colander Calendar   34
A Line for Whatever   35
The City Poet's Line   36
Warming My Hands Over Words   37
In Confidence   38
A Pant on Fire   39
Cocoon-toon   40
Title Bouts   41
Postmodern Martial Arts   42

Challenge and Response   43

Brush Work   43
Cornerstone for Misery   44
World Series   45
In River City   46
Fright or Flight   47
Volunteer Heroes   48
Pepperoni Peace   49
The Wait for Lame Excuses   50
Country Folklore   51
The Tremor State   52
A Quilting Lullaby   53
The Snake on the Lawn   54
To Good Wealth   55
The Galvanized Steeles   56
Tallman   57
The Shame of It All   58
Safe Passage   59
Police Convention   60

Treasure / Trash   61

Tortoises   61
Chew, Chew, Chew   62

Gullet Gulch   63

Human Resources Department   64

The Log Jam   65

With Matching Cheers   66

The Church Lot   68

The Law and the Crooked   70

City Welfare   71

The Astrodome   72

Practically Addicted   73

Cables Home   74

The Yankee at Home   75

The Baggage Claim   76

The Paper Cup World   77

And Every Day Is a Hard Head Day   78

Standard Royal Flush   79

The Empty Busy Time Bomb   80

The Cameo Crowd   81

Now Clones   82

Acknowledgments   83

About the Author   84

This book is dedicated to my sisters
Maureen and Kathleen

City Slicker

"The trees encountered on a country stroll
Reveal a lot about that country's soul."

W. H. Auden

Western State Penitentiary

Entering the prison yard
by way of the womb
and leaving only as the fertilizer
for another civilization, first
the inmate toddles the grounds,
Columbus, Magellan.

He conquers his mother's reach
and his father's nature,
while planting his standard in the hands
of convicted murderers and rapists.

To ease his Atlas shoulders,
the natives prod him to where
the birds soar above a hut:
He has since flapped his arms
to the thought of freedom.

Leading his private expeditions
to death's wall and to the curly locks
of the electrified mob,
he returns to the promises
iron balls deeded in the dust,
to the gates from which he came.

In the body salt on the grounds
beneath him, he tangles his feet
in longitude and latitude
so that he may eat where beyond
the topsoil traps for millennia
captured claws and paws.

Upon the mesh of rooted bones
he lumps himself, a stone
for crows, exotic dreams, and crimes
that only demise forgives.

Anthem

From the mountains of wheat
to unmined coasts of milk and money
thoughts are empty of wailing bellies.

The air is grimy with snacks and booze
on the fat that belches townhouse and ranch
and movement cripples a creeping hand
while rocketing chains and expensive pain.

Among cropless bowls and wilting bodies
wall-to-wall living rooms a moment away are dragged
but not a kernel is shaken from wallpaper eyelids
left with magazine pinups selling soap.

In the churches of cones, gingerbread, and beans
the dieting and lonely gathering mid-week
cover their mouths with bored hands
and cups of decaf coffee.

Viva Viva

The explorers of backyards
and entrepreneurs of suburban boredom
vacation Las Vegas
tangled in the safety net
its knitters proclaim the United States.

Risking little more than breathing,
the owners of nine-to-five pockets and rawhide
have long since lost the blood and bone
of Lewis, Clark, and Betsy Ross.

Corralled by tinsel and bandits at the airport terminals,
the low vaulting trampolinist from Sacramento
and the quiet Salvation Army tambourinist from Miami
stampede through the chute of the brass ring
and neon silver dollars.

The casinos' arms mine the last nickel
from the cookie jar brokers and the nightclub
dancers while tumbling the amateur acrobats dry.
Clothesline daredevils land on their backs
in their workweek beds, mulling
the disaster of a missing shirt.

New Species

The uncarved states bucked
beneath the net of highways;
the European hunters of circus animals
drove futile stakes against
the kicking geology and humping topography.

Dizzying the dinosaur,
the occidental hulk posed
for the two-dimensional fisherman's mind
and from its volcanic skin
spouts entertainment for itself.

Unearthing the conical future
from the ore of living emotion,
the curious seers construct fossils
somewhere on a continental shelf.

No vampire, no spectacle for wagon or tent;
thoughts, similar in nature, run wild
across a land's hide eluding the ghosts
that apple for apple fall.

Exterior Wash

We bless then groom our escape
vehicles with undercoating and wax
sealer, while sitting at the controls,
mangy from boredom, mangled
by our lack of reflection.

The mountains of refuse we've left
behind, our trails of grime, have led
to these attempts to cover our tracks
with ritual and shine. Behind
our innocence, our experience
speeds toward the rest area.

Every success at evading
responsibility for landfill
is rewarded with rust and the broken
destination that becomes us.
Considering every passing glare,
we avoid the bridge abutment
and the push and pull
of internal combustion,
but we are hauled away by the mirror,
the wind praising our hair.

The Bomb

Having mixed explosive amounts
of gasoline, rubber, and steel,
we sit idle among the wheels of automobiles
in parking lots that burst to junkyards
and cemeteries – "whichever arrives first."

With our fingers in our ears, we do not sense
homes and industrial parks that teeter
on curbstones, and the city's rubble
bouncing to the shopping mall.

We had hoped to conquer earth's nomenclature,
to hold our love at bay on lover's leap.

When the Los Angeles bus settles
with Jones' great grandchildren
and safety pins hold a hem and hmm together,
we won't be lone gone into the country.

We descend from the architect's skyline
into the crater of NYC. Our city planners
in a shade of blue surround us
with their guns drawn against the bottlenecks
of refined fossil fuel.

The Service Station's Island

Surrounded by their ocean of asphalt,
the islands of civilized derricks, windshield wash,
and oily rags are hundreds of slick rainbows
away from the grease monkey's bay.

Singing to hulls that wreck themselves
at curbs around a corporation's private property,
the full-figured pumps with their hands in their hair
or in a washed up heap's pockets
are said to cause the accidents of warriors
sailing home from Troy Toy Co.,
Persian Rug Inc., etc.

The masts are tied to their sailors
while Simonize wax fills caves and wrinkles.
The commuter rolls a tire past colorful displays
swearing an oath for old Tahiti,
a hallucination down the road
after One Martini Drive.

Par for the Course

One bedroom community hole
and putting green is indistinguishable
from the next, and drunk-driven carts
roll from office traps
into each neighborhood's streets.
Lawn ornaments mark carpets
that lead to where a cup prepares for its fill.

On the first fairway Mrs. Smith
sinks a pink flamingo's leg
while the corner of a gopher's eye weeds.

At the eighteenth tee and green
Ms. Jones pins a bird bath and wind wheel
to snag and hold Whitman hackers
buzzing about bouquets and bottles.

The poor Does tangled outside these links,
turn tires into daisy gardens
or put Madonnas in bathtubs to stun
all but the Rips from dust bowls
that Jane and John call home.

Bear Right and Keep to the Left

The berth along the normal expressway
allows for most everybody in lanes to pass.
On the way to the cemetery,
roadside rest stops run quick quizzes,
and often hand out certificates
or strap boarding house beds to backs.
From cry baby to pigeon hole hospice,
the I Witness Institute operates
to impress traffic lights
behind such enemy lines as
"I celebrate myself, and sing myself,"
"I saw the best minds of my generation,"
Neighbors get Bonnie and Clyde wherever,
or the drone heard buries with cross hairs.
Harboring within Miss Manner
or convening beneath pinstripe jargon,
a citizen docile but capable carries on ideology
without stripping the median.
Without exit, the well-contained vehicles
maintain the surfaces with crushed bone
on clover leaf or straight-away.
The toll road ends the green project
at the jaded crescent among fallow fellows
with faults put on the line
for the one last scream role.

The Pin Up Girls

Hope and Joy collect stamps
while disappointment owns the calendar.
Children hopscotch through the decades,
where in the schoolhouse
custodians salvage the threads
through experience. The lesson
is repeated, while with tweezers,
magnifying glass, and a lamp,
the classes ignore the teacher
and turn possessions this way and that.
The ends loom as Penny braids yarns
into whispers when the folk fall asleep.
(The colors taint goods, but the background
smudges the angry footprints by poets.)
Xs mark the sport for the treasure seeker
late again. In the recesses,
the explorers see the horizon all around,
the last hoopla hoop undefeated.
Nothing personal in the sunrise
or yesterday. The albums burst
with postage from as far away as Mars
and June doesn't give a hoot.

American Gothic, Circa 1950, by Rote

Slippers, curiosity and desire,
buff the polish of exurban floors
for the ancient arrogance of newspapers
stinking of violence and retaliation.

The dog, kicked from the yard
to the lots of a city's shelter,
foraged beaches with friends and fauna
before the perverted questioner.

The pipe, for example, loot of this victor,
carries the peace of one relieved
and content to impress accidental facts
with the color and volume of Sunday comic strips

for the memory of other gullible travelers
who grow miles into their contempt for nature.

American Dream

The home movie of the fenced-in green
surrounding a house of sticks puts
a nation to sleep so that if anyone wakes
he is without the bacon to buy back his life.

Franklin's promise of original self-crafted
Homo sapiens was buried among pages
of fiction to be disinterred by desperate
shovelers. Mass produced husbands

and wives spray lacquer on each
of the conveyer belt's children and lose
them on continental shelves. The people
of ceramic molds fear the feeling of

their bodies in their hands in order to keep
a thought of their own from adding or subtracting.
Too few lumps of clay from the land of the free
find their way to a hand of the brave.

American Dream Extended

The house wrenches us from weather
and fastens us to a location.
If you prefer an air of indifference
and distance from places to which
you once moved close, then this tool
won't serve your will. Your screws
must be loose, but down the road
a shirt and hat would bring
you to your country of comfort.
The instrument with which we are stuck
towels us dry, shades us cool,
and embraces us warm,
so we might maximize our grip
on each moment without it addressing us
as though we had handles, purpose.
Fixed to a spot that repairs to a plot,
we are easy to find by anyone
interested in the bulls' eyes of the bedroom.
Though, these dramas and minor adjustments
require our mastery of the equipment,
the heroic lots of the craftsman
and tight quarters are full of life.
It is during the tension of our torque,
when castles become overalls
or when the dust balls
become tumbleweed in rooms,
that we remember that the devices
in belts on our hips are also in our boxes
and now may be the time to use our hands
on some other kind of shelter.

From Valley to Valet

Rolling out their hot top nature onto the rainbow,
doormen carpet earth
with ribbons of black destinations.

With nowhere exotic to go on rubber and oil,
dignitaries parade up and down parking lots
as remembered roses, flamingos on marshlands,
and in the evening float through each street's tube
of fluorescent light, shadows.

Between the sun and the flat device that sucks
its heat where no fauna props a fawn suspended
by gold threads, master and servant, sharing
the same flesh, stand in wind waiting to have
their dreams thrashed from their hulls
between hard and difficult darknesses.

Creating the way to the materialized human soul
from naked hunger among weeds and beasts,
restless workers open doors to extinction
and their blood, deaths whose rotting will matter only
to the eight ball side of a visionary's putting green.

Historical Data

The historian's every period
draws a black shroud around
the industrious worker's
attempt to stack bound odds
in favor of colorful flags
carried by innovators scaling crises.

When the poet's wild end of the line
finally meets chugging wheels of civilization,
momentum clears a short thoughtless way
upon the heave of a dilemma.

The journalist's skin crawls
from the wreck to a blurred news photo
of the scholar's first aid,
while survivors scatter into their old age,
tooting their whistles at dream cows.

The path cleared by words "steel"
and "steam," America's attitude
about people driven westward
was simply too much, so the idea of Eden
still, hissing, fades, an accordion
on a hill in Virginia, Indiana, Oregon.

The Head of Man

"a universe entirely possessed and occupied by human life,
a city of which the stars are suburbs"

Northrop Frye

To fix eyes in their lamp sockets
against the stationary night,
we pave the earth.

Along expressways to the parking lot,
limbless lashes are strung
with electrical wires of wonder.

The road crews ride planes of asphalt
and rope straying steering wheels
to follow detour cones.

The explosive idea of tar and feathering
the mammoth rock, followed by graders
and rollers, pulverized "nest" and "lair"
and led to the elixir accented suburbanite.

Staring down the constellations
in its hunt for something more handsome,
the ambivalent head of civilization
resting upon the shoulders of its road
finds it admires the long spaces between stars.

Masked forests and marshes pretend to cue
soliloquies, but the alien face has numbed
the monkey into its inhuman sleep.

Orbital Dating Game

In the Goldie Locks zone
even the brunette eats her porridge
and thanks her lucky star:
Earthlings feel Grace around.
Great Bear claws hibernate,
while just beyond jewel moderation,
the space tresses brush extravagant.
Woe, the scent from last night
in public places puts smiles on faces.
A'nt Sophie crawls around
her hill conserving energy and conducts
her wedding at the local American Legion.
Tectonic plates shift bottoms
while waiting for the oven or refrigerator
to eat girls sleeping in beds.
Should everything go just right,
a rock for ages, attracted by a sunrise,
noon, and sunset, will continue to dance
on the run, celebrating the breaking
and entering by flowing solar waves.
If in another forest a hungry
and tired leggy Laurel seeks solace
on a fence between hell
and the Ice Capades, the glass eyes
sent into galactic sockets may tell her
with a wink and flair. Then the blonde
wonder boy would leap about the discovery
and exploit: perhaps "Florida
retirement community all life long."
Until then, Little Lord Blunder Roy
takes credit for telling
good fortune with silver spoons.

Lawn Art

"3D Life Size Flamingos

This realistic life-size flamingo pair will add a splash of color to that special spot in your yard or garden. Easily make them from layers of wood, steel rods (four 1/2 inch diameter x 36 inch long) and our full-size pattern. The largest flamingo is 44 inches tall."

Brush with Exposure

The path to trust troubles footing,
lashes eyes with jetted tendrils.

Each step in the manual for the ability
to be vulnerable includes no directions.

Flagstones, one-legged pink flamingoes,
or the Virgin in an upended bath tub

camouflages shame from curb
to front door, behind which secrets fester.

Judges stand at every window
with megaphones and sit idling

in police cruisers pointing fingers.
Balance and the willingness to share

any berth along the way doesn't clear
thicket but provides shoulders

and similar stories. For instance, race
and sexuality may slow the engendering

blame game to a joke. Keys to assurance lock
nothing but open to revise, revise, revise.

The Blotter

Bringing paper to ink
that engulfs the room,
the poet holds his breath
and waits for dawn.

Take any coal miner, psychologist,
from any crowd and he sleeps
dreaming, digging for a moon
to glimpse beyond himself.

When the yellow ball discovers
and breaks the window,
technicians are picking daisies
with a glove in a field.

The schoolhouse empties by a door
for a moment of fresh air, the lesson,
before the children hang themselves
back in their closets.

A mole in the bell of a tuba,
the student of horror, flees
the orchestrated pit
so he may translate the first letter
of the wind's soliloquy.

Movers

Though we carry our grand pianos
through each day, we never learn to play.

With the maestro, a nimble wind
over taut guts, each lesson proves
much too expensive.

We poke chopsticks and bow
elephantine at the jeers
from the other Bach broken ivory luggers.

Maneuvering from our beds beneath
the starless belly of our harp-hidden para-box,
we wrestle with Mozart,
roll over Beethoven, and rest
our bones to balance the lodes.

Daily, the dark linings of thunderstorms
sprinkling and pounding on the ends
of the keyboards are guaranteed
and not optional for our wooden-lidded limousines.

With no surgery able to remove the hunch,
we demonstrate our distance from paradise
but claim the cathedral in our image.

In the evening, sheet music,
tucked around a candelabrum
for the would-be vocalist, weighs too much
and into silent dreams we are crushed.

Pedestrian Poets

Pushed along by momentary winds,
we find anything of the old in the new.
Baby, pinned but flailing,
grasps because it gasped
at the way back to the uterus,
and the old man detects a schoolboy
friend in a defective doorknob.

Wobbling upon two sentimental sensations
while creating the self's epic poem,
the wandering matters also occasionally scratch
at their incomplete and balding interpretations.

Understanding only fragmented images
and similes, our gathering of objective
correlative verses soon fall separate.

We arrange enough novelty
to sleep part of the night
and cross our fingers for as long as we can.

When we discover something
of our first breath in our lungs' last letting go,
each laureate leaves the linking of first
and last metaphors to unexplainable rot.

Courtship

The pubescent lad spreads
the asphalt picnic-blanket
and uses heart-shaped suburbs
to hold the corners from the wind.

Burdened with the basket,
the lass rests in the center
of love's unconsciousness
and arranges the conversation
into streets and parking lots and plazas.

The two workers, sprawling
among the plates and utensils,
feed each other and play
until sandwiched between two black sheets
and then catch a bus for the city limits.

When love is a steel erection under glass,
the evening does not reveal the heaves
and pots and blades of grass:
Perfect places are interrupted
by the clumsy feet of a poem sweet poem.

Monument Boulevard Vacation

Celebrating victory,
the lazy racist generals
lean against granite
along the boulevard
in a city from where
veranda squatters
fled with mint juleps.
The bronze horses
keep watch over black faces
without a county, or income
long after the uniform blue
rode through planting flags.
In the suburban strongholds,
where forces plot against
a tennis player
and boys and girls
sharing humiliation
with a father, a mother,
shameless children
pretend integration.
A dominion state
frustrates education
and encourages guns and liquor
on a Sunday despair
to distract a focus from subterfuge
by listless imaginations.
Come, the harmony tears
at first glance,
but few militants in other states
or outside limits pass an eye.

The Twain Shall Meet

Jim shared the school room floor
with Huck who majored in Scapegoat
and earned more wisdom than
any Finn. When that dawn arrived
for the student and night and day
played with the Mississippi,
a Native American used that golden
rule in an attempt to teach
Europe and Asia the way:
Potash on Planet Ltd. thrust into space
along with all the good days to die.
Joe gave and gave and gave up
but the contribution stashes in pouches.
Tom continues to hoard and waste
without detention and without regard
for progeny. Becky put out
the trash each week but never
the source. The American speaks mutt,
by definition desperate for unity.
Citizens suppose that is why the bark
leaves teeth marks in legs.

Sounding From St. Petersburg, Missouri

Before departing Camp America
for the wilderness, the scout leader,
Mr. Sawyer, filched history homework
and moral compasses from backpacks.
Orienting the troop toward replacing
teeth with whitewashed picket fences,
the prankster counts blessings a sawbuck
at a time. Marlow the Midwesterner
consults a spiritual eminence,
any multi-national corporation.
An alpha-male for Becky makes a way
in the god-dang world by forcing unity
on progeny. Of thunder and lightning,
Shakespeare and company drew lines
in sand and stone, bringing tribes
nose to nose. Injun Joe and Jim drone
that prime rib from Genesis
now hangs in a store window, sausages.
The lookout patrols grunt on and on.

Portal Properties

An artist digs the rabbit hole that ends up
surprising pedestrians and patrons
with here and then there.
The entrances and exits dot cultures,
extending and infesting tradition.

Tunneling through top soil,
beneath pottery, and architecture,
around blocks and class roots
toward the language in evolution.

Audiences plan on the same old
bedrock and touchstone
and a little change with which to purchase
beer in the evening.
The latest technology, fad, and cool aid
spice spectator lives walking the street
before nine and after five.

Dinner contains all the necessary taste:
steak and small fry who report on sports.
Jack Rabbit complains with buckshot
that left behind means: Sculpture sits
at a fault, painting colors darken day,
and poetry twists mean.

Eighteen holes for golf and yet
the magician reaches into a top hat.
Ahead by a nose whisker,
the ears deliver a puff-ball to market.

Now, The Fashion Celebrity

Collecting reports from senses,
the spinning wheel looms.
The fibers tangling into thread
include the unconscious records
as well as might be.

Without a spindle each faculty
roams alone, even at home.
Quicker than ticker-tape
and no thicker than silk,
the present slips into something
more comfortable, and the spider
backs into a corner once again.
Yet, a spool will pause to put
the evidence in order, even if
the participant must live in the past
with the paparazzi.

That's Precision

Rehearsing their song and dance
each morning for a show
that never takes place, neighborhoods
long to kick their cans
onto the Broadway stage.

The alarm clocks, toasters,
and traffic lights build chords,
produce bodies of noise
in orchestra pits
of the off Broadway theatres
while performers on the spot
read their lines from a script.

Amateur shows, mimicking
the marquee's electric constellations
on factory floors and in business
office routines, attempt to keep
the audience of playwrights
and critics from the bedroom scenes.

The members of troupes
flip, flop, and must come home
to Closet Drama Drive, Prologos Lane,
Soliloquy Street, to play straight-men
for any lampooner's steely barbs
and to eat their crow
when slipping into their crowded beds.

Salesmen waltz their Olivier
while their immortality
is discovered in a gong and hook
adlibbing the punch lines
of denouement (z.z.z.)
twisted within two sheets.

Hot House Homes

In their pots beneath a glassy sky,
children wear their ribbons
into foyers and parlors as do the trunks
of trowel-shaped leaves still around them.

Tangling its roots toward the water table
and stretching its uppermost tendrils
for its share of sun, the rural vegetation
crawls and sprints, climbs and burrows,
pruned only by the space between the stars.

The crotches that hold nests beneath
the backyard's white-washed magnifying
glass would tumble against a wind or fry
beneath industrial acid, a dried weed on sand.

Deep in the darkest thickets of concrete
and asphalt, where humans are most themselves,
the lion and war elephants roll in and trample
flowers to feed on each other's carcass
and to water themselves beside
the artificial rubber tree.

Ivy and Norfolk pines witness, here,
the construction of greenhouses and their malls
before returning wealthier from the paws
and maws to the slow cooking of a TV screen.

Neither Rhyme nor Season

The untimely artistic energy gushes
from wells drilled with great regret
miles below the tourist industries.
Souvenir shops and motels
occupy the tuned in hearts
thumping to mouth-watering iambs
on pop stations. Refineries
for raw talent stockpile ambition
and sublimation for cities and suburbs
that tour universities and Hallmark
for factory prints. Every means
has been tried and every expense
continues in an attempt
to stem at its human source the accident
spewing with paint, ink, noise, even stone
at a studio here and writing desk there.

The unrecognizable products
from dispersant sheen teens
and tar-balled gunk punks
carry regret boons and exotic sorrow
as the thrill babies thrill using thumbs
and temp-jobs to paper over
the oops career destined to hang
on a bank vault wall in fifty years.
Plumes from the slick poetry pipe
stop as natural gas in each exhales,
but not without the disaster welling up
in someone else deep beneath
the marketing hustle bustle
punching holes in fin and flesh.

Capital's Colander Calendar

Camouflaged by capitalism,
the when for art never arrives.
The staff notes commuter rails
in the parallel universe.
American duck hunters
buy the fall phalanx in oil
to match the living room couch.
The Dutch pull Rembrandt canvases
to the chin for the night chill
while the French mine Cezanne
during the day.
The scheduled profound caesura
evacuates the platform – et tu brute.
Any large print in sculpture
feels geek to people
creeping around in new shoes.
Impromptu sublime beatings
escape the gallery roamers.
Tiffany frames epiphany
for the police dragnet.
Education by hunger
translates with ease into greed
when the belly fills,
and everyone in the orchestra
plays the dog whistle,
until the audience howls.

A Line for Whatever

The American poet dots hamburgers
with his blood at the drive-thru window.
Napkins absolve words
that may slip from the corners
of his mouth. A squeeze bottle
farts and sputters intention.

The procession of disposable families
idles and crawls in each aerodynamic
bragging rite of urbane grease.
On their way to the bone yard,
where they become the fast food
for worms, whatever the unsuspecting
vampires say is said in commodity, fashion.

Beyond plastic and dumpsters,
capes and teeth huddle beneath the neon light,
each ignoring the shivers of others:
Anything the size of suburbia
is hunted for its ermine and mink.

When he is fired or grows up,
Anonymous ceases his offer, "French
fries with that?" and gets his moment
in the line citizens don't decipher.

The City Poet's Line

Cliffs of glass and bluffing air
surround the witnessing pedestrians
with hunger and soot: the poet cleans windows.

Lathering upper-lips and chins
of the architect's pigeon holes,
the barber bleeds private visions
with a rubber blade while conversing
with a millennium.

Swashbuckling the urge to build illusion
from bystanders and clerks,
the pirate of pupils with a surgeon's precision
swings his sword in the rigging,
piling the curtain on a drifting deck.

The mountaineer of edifices and facades
clears a foothold in the artifice
and descends the I-beam's tall tale
until all feet are on the ground
and every head leans upon his rag.

Warming My Hands Over Words

With each fresh sheet
cold enough to cover my face,
page upon page of winter
has set itself in front of me
and published my doodle,
my stick man print.

Though I'm up to my bifocals in manuscript,
my impressions of angels
and wide winged rainbows seem worth
repeating here as are the primitive love letters
left at a woman's feet to illustrate
my virile ability to backtrack.

Not so very far into the rings
of this shaved white pine log before me,
my deliberate ink demands attention:
Poems into the neighboring woods,
and autobiographical novels of my automobile
all ways, with convention coming to mind.

While this snow storm bears
the same Greek column engraving as others,
the carrot and coal want to speak
for the body of literature behind it,
want passersby to remember the confetti
of polar circles we become.

In Confidence

The poem assures the columnist
that each foot steps forward
while by the yard the backhoe
piles images to either side.
Earth drops off behind the reader.
Scenic mountains with cave-dwelling
earth worms sandwich
the riddle fiddler by lunch time.
However, the paving stones
encourage a plodding along
by newspaper bathers
and novel romance dreamers
who never go home again.
Even the manual marvel
recognizes a short-cut
to ancient Greece.
The gravedigger knows
a hole when dug though.
And the craters and hills
tell a story also, a chorus
mouthing something with curled lips.
On the sunny side, somewhere,
remember that within the anthology
trunks stamp in defiance on leaves.

A Pant on Fire

Whether on a stroll
alone to the corner store
or dining out with friends,
fictions shelter
each liar from the reign.
(The compositions tiff.)
Opened novels
build seven gables
for the adults
while the children
perch beneath propped pretend.
Every hand releases
daily public relations
rumors into the ears so that
the parade evades with a hero.
A fake limp wins
the beggar another meal.
When the sky falls,
umbrellas save the day.
Into nowhere, opinion
drives the expert
to frisk facts for faith.
Eternal life and "me"
can't handle the weather.
Should the outrageous
threat meet feet with a rock,
witnesses arrive with newspaper,
rulers, and gods.

Cocoon-toon

Wound in slumbers spun from the silk
of single family homes, Disney World children
hang at the end of Western Civ. 2000 –
Goofy, Dumbo, and Dopey.

Through adulthood into the riskless dizziness
of angels without the actual laughter
of a meadow's colors, the suburban
larvae swing in career hammocks,
the sense's nectar decaying in buds
and on the wind.

The forest, permitting the crawl
into death beds, flutters its vast verdure,
rocks the cradle while poking the bundle
in its ribs: "you, on the twisted branch."

Only the snapping of technology's tendrils,
leaving disaster's babes in burning cities,
would stimulate the inhibiters of transformation
so that ranch houses stick their necks out
and the sky spreads its wealth.

Title Bouts

Each canvas compress
never stopped a bleeding.

A moment in the life
of the artist's exposed nerve
throbs on a wall, giving birth
to its wound in a crowd
vulnerable to perform first aid in a gallery.

Where there is little success
doctors and nurses go about their business
as bystanders matching colors,
bumping into forms, fading into old age
with picture frames under their arms.

Yet, any healing by artists would be
an art dealer's nightmare,
and all museum egresses would spill
back into the sports complex
as though from locker rooms.

Any competition winner is a chump
who gets stretched on a gauze pad
before brushing himself off and getting up.

Postmodern Martial Arts

With what we don't have flaunted all around.
Gnats taunting garbage. False sincerity
igniting rats. Gucci, Gucci goo. Malaise
stuck on the heel of a shoe fills nostrils.
Gross domestic happiness
waves its mortgage to waive fear
for mayonnaise. The flow charts.
Feet look sewer. Acquisitions and enjoyments
rev their motives while waiting for the third
generation cowboy. "Come down off a cloud
named Silver." US cash total 300,000 =
the 150 million meek. What's wrong
with the unimaginative tells the street people
how lucky the dead are not. Earth
my word my witness. Deregulated violence
drones it Tasers: gawking testicles,
not Moloch moms spoiling dinner,
children, and their own lives. Get hip
and walk a mile. The beat survives
on bread alone. Too late to wake up man.
The buses for one leave their curves.
The dear in headlights pushes hope
with its eye out all made up.

Challenge & Response

"Civilizations may be likened to companions of 'Sleepers of Ephesus' who have just risen to their feet and have started to climb on up the face of the cliff."

Arnold Toynbee

Brush Work

Greeting nature's gloves
across our cheeks with a grin
and a hoe, we soon don
the businessman's strait-jacket.

The circle of unemployed movie stars
around a fire in a deep forest
scares the swan from leaving
any stone undisturbed.

When hunters flock
to public gardens looking
for something to push around,
they find Howdy Doody and strings
to the mysterious continent that a mirror
or lagoon are quicker voyages to.

Once upon the finger peninsulas
of a reflected technician
and upon hearing his untangled wind,
the Columbus will eat an aborigine.

Cornerstone for Misery

Crossed fingers and buckled knees
hold breath and then crawl
worry stones until eyelids crack
storm clouds and fists pound Earth.
Better to plow through tomorrow
emptying seeds from a sack
without looking back. Better
to wear the bald head or carry
a leg in a bucket and celebrate
what limps along in the rain.
Better to allow the unicorn room
to vanish from the lexicon.
Better to reach for the empty sky
with steel and glass and not
grub in the dirt while waiting
for lightning to enlighten.

World Series

"That's where the economic and political empowerment of the
developing world – the 'rise of the rest' as I call it – comes in"

Fareed Zakaria

Pitched until the mantle collapsed,
the two trophies disappeared beneath
jet engines and 3000 bodies.
iPhones in hands, "Why me?"
stepped from taxi cabs in suits
and shoes that shine. In league,
the world without a New York City
suffered schadenfreude in the dark.
Team America cried foul, and alarmed
referees chased the remote control pilot
and the drones into caves. A decade
later, bronze horns wreathing
Wall Street melted into tears
for the taxpayer robbed by bankers,
and Asia jumped the starter gun
when airlifted cash on pallets landed
a baton. A relay circles the Earth.
The rest that rises in steel
and glass sees nothing to learn;
the sun casts light just so.

In River City

As the sky falls, you don't notice
your deeper breath, nor your head
more often in a cloud watching birds
with a star in your eye. Even

the whistling is not the velocity
of anything concrete but your
wisdom showing up for work
another day. Your new blue hat

cocked to the side placing all blame
where it belongs looks spiffy to
the nihilist. You greet other circus
tent poles going about the business

of human beings, even though
the silver lining causes the collapse
of knees and then the ring masters.
With no place for ticker tape, the solar

system meets, billiards in motion on cue,
you and your progeny with a nickel
in a pocket stir in the dream of a droplet
on the brow of a lucky asteroid.

Fright or Flight

Citizens of secret cities polish floors
beneath their beds with the crisp fronts
of shirts. Skies of springs and foam
held up by posts and frames never rain

and no god sags in the clouds drawing
the wrath of outdoor threats. The snow
of interiors piles high in shoes. Bootstraps
are put to rest. The safety first students

graduated from under desks and frequent
fliers shifted their compartments from
between their knees. Chased by a sense
of fear, mop heads show up for work

and crawl after paychecks. Backbones
of dust cloths never stood against evil's
thin air in an epoch of blue capes
and telephone booths on every corner;

two sets of neighboring eyes have
never confronted each other at
the attitude of between five and six feet.

Volunteer Heroes

Need's basic training has
always supported the troops.
Bellies order boys and girls to shoplift
for rations until despairing parents
march families into the firing range.

Three square meals a day
and a tent propped by oil barrels
rescue refugees from crossfire –
better than a cellmate, a guard,
and a tray through a door.

The misfortune of birth mows the troops down
before an enemy training its sights.
The drill sergeant's larynx wouldn't swell
with anger if his platoon were more
want of an upper class conviction.

But entitlement camps demonstrate
their appreciation by hiding on weekends
in exurban tool sheds. Other mornings,
phalanxes of ungrateful voters storm
the cities by way of gasoline stations,

one soldier to a Humvee
while poor blood spills into each tank.

Pepperoni Peace

When delivering democracy
from 10,000 feet, purveyors know
all parties below tip and receive a slice
straight from the oven
without a chance to scatter.
But then, before hell rang the doorbell,
the men mixing tomato sauce
in the kitchens on foundations
had addresses to populations
and orders also: The pot
had been simmering
to a boil a long time.
Pizzazz thrown in the air
sits flat with extra cheese
or the works on top in a box.
When the lid flies open,
the smell is unmistakable:
Nothing sells like the sell in the morning.
On paper, the meal with map and driver
could feed the world and may,
even considering home-made concoctions
ready to spice up the messengers.
The average citizen dipping
a finger in the tomatoes and oregano
casts a vote and everybody else knows.
The dough spreads around
when everyone thinks
about a pie peace.
Burnt remnants fade from memory.

The Wait for Lame Excuses

The lopsided war
between the tribal
and infantilized peoples
continues until the men
with spears, spare time,
and misogyny wound themselves.
The lollipop populations
hand out diapers
to hunters in slings.
The happy ending
that thumb suckers demand
comes in various flavors,
but it arrives.
Asymmetrical gangsters
gather here and there in the hills
to lob disasters
when schoolyards fill
so that lessons lapse unlearned.
Hopscotch and jackstones
pass the time for fabled hares
who wait for accidental injury.
When Brute Billy comes
looking for first aid,
the conflict subsides
and Nancy Nurse Coerce cuts
a deal so that the nap mats
absorb another playmate
with a life expectancy.

Country Folklore

The beheaded government ran around
the barnyard squirting bullets and blood.
With the oven heating up, the farmer and wife
absorbed the violence and dressed dinner.
After the religious Feast of St. Loot,
the occupying army put its feet
up on the table and picked its teeth
until insurgents hear belching
and the coup backfired. Sweetbread
and neck bones boil in a soup
that has every liberated citizen treading broth.
How did the country with its range,
mountains, forest, and fields become
someone's recipe for just desserts?
What hunger do big shots aim to satisfy?
Questions grumble in the gullets
of herds and milkers. Neighbors
and folks from nearby towns smell
the quagmire stew of ambushes
and convoys and cross borders to the ladle.
Fools with explosive news want a piece
of the passion. The new host and hostess
greet the parties with disaster.
Seats at the peace table need to be dredged
from a swamp of body parts.

The Tremor State

The tanks citizens get for participating
in government remain camouflaged.
The landscape shifts roadside to roadside,
foot to foot. Architecture with the frieze
turns attention before the edifice artifice:
nihilism bursting concrete on the scene.
Neighborhoods scatter in all directions.
Rear guards to families shake tools
at the advancing thunder and lightning strikes.
A storm taints towns dead.
The clean slate upon which injustice
marks lessons in one-sided etiquette
smoulders around body parts and bulldozers.
Unfurling a refugee camp against
the howling change, NGOs patch
a pock in a heritage bleeding out:
Fabric unravels to dam the survivors.
The untouched pressure points
rumble anywhere surrounded in steel.

A Quilting Lullaby

Manufacturing the thread of history
while hoarding comforting patches of earth,
we then sow seams of a guilt.

Waiting for a rescue by angels,
we eye the needle, and our stitches do
not give to cold boney feet
that seem to grow to be our own.

Buried alive in our heirloom
to hold it close against the chill of each day,
we slaughter gravesite vandals.

The weavers without uniform
stands at attention still as barbarians
rush in around them and for warmth
build fires from street corners.

We sing our anthem and pray to go to sleep
huddled against the continuing winter,
our hair growing wild with lice.

The Snake on the Lawn

Having bitten the coasts with its utility poles
and parted the territory between
with its mapped slither, the road
now winds around the ribcage of home.

The oceans of air that once crashed
upon a house, meadow, and wood,
have been routed, crushed into air conditioners.

Now, a mashed apple upon the school's
asphalt blackboard, Earth has been bottled,
oblivion's note to the sprawling metropolis
that suffers its own comfort.

With every squirm in the neighborhoods' beds,
parents separate and move next door:
love scrambles each time the car radio stops.

To Good Wealth

Each day, the self-administered placebos
change nothing for the culture.
The prescriber knows the patient well.
Druggists get something for nothing.
Phew, the fever weakens the immune
system for walking pneumonia.
Uncle Pennybags continues to lead
democracy around by the nose
to wherever the powerless can't afford
to go. Needles and pins numb
the citizens into patience.
Even the creative class can't transform
finding the sublime in payment;
brown paper bags worn require eyeholes.
Well, enough to go to jail or pace
the boardwalk, an immigrant
from the Baltics swallows the cure.

The Galvanized Steeles

I-beams make up flesh,
bone, and neurons of people
such as you and the generation of me.
The awkward faces and rigid backs
give away the pile-driving
activities of infancy.

Toddlers follow the blueprints
of parental architects.
Blah, blah, blah heated
at high temperatures can be
poured to form an ego

though strangers haunt the expanse
of inner space green
for fingerprints.

Rivets and welds
cuff the weaknesses
of desire and fear:
Joints joined with joists.

Cranes, genomic scaffolding tip and totter
while tribes of construction crews

iiiiiiiIiiiiiiiIiiiiiiIiiiiiiIiiiiiI

stutter an utter, each introducing
alpha shells, beta shelves, iota salves.
Tugging cables in hope of a puppeteer,
the steel worker balances on a dot
or stands sandwiched between horizontal bars
to reassure that subconscious
sheets are beneath.

Tallman

Standing upon the sun's rocky shoulders,
the balancing biped waves
his tools at his problems
before encasing the instruments as trophies.

His troubles convinced him of his great stature,
as though they were stars
over his head keeping him on his toes.

Tearing at the raw material,
bruising the brows of his green monster,
the handyman forgot how much of an insect he is
beneath the patent leather sky.

When his acrobatic tricks
heap Mr. Tallman at the hooves
of discarded how-to manuals
with the light bulb unchanged, perhaps then
poetry will rest its bare rays upon his head.

The Shame of It All

In hands the planet buried its terrain
and turns to the stars for constellation.

Itself poked at, the devoted moon
offers its craters.

Winking, yet on their best behavior,
the stellar hug promises nothing
and demonstrates the reflecting body.

The critical eye, focusing
through the ozone,
radiates the skyscrapers
and scorches mines.

Beneath two palms,
the clay was pushed into chin and cheeks,
gouged by thumbs into eye sockets,
and squeezed by fingers
into cauliflower and a nose.

Soon, in a global, rose-tinted atrium,
Earth rolls its eyes, its I,
toward the other stones of the solar system
set glittering in a waiting room.

Safe Passage
For Mahmud Sadeghi

Refugees once reported America
extended an arm with an umbrella
over nations where bullets reigned.
Later, moving targets disclosed
huddles from the threatening storm
clouds and gave Colossus thanks
for living up to the reputation.
When the canopy ribs stretched
newspapers too many decades,
the Green Giant appeared
to have talons and stolen from friends.
Days for spine and poses seemed
to collapse into a shuffle, stage right.
Now, China mocks with one hundred
Manhattans. Islamic fighters imitate
multi-national corporations.
Sweatshop voodoo doll pin cushions
distribute well in the outer reaches.
The pig pile origin will snort
until Nemesis and Atlas allow
a titan to stand in a harbor once more.

Police Convention

Eyes and ears locate and identify
misbehavior and apply
the appropriate institution.
Drones tag with labels rebellion
in the spleen or with arms.
If not video cameras, then the sleeping
commuter taking the subway
should prompt docile but capable
from the punk with the spray paint.
The slums fill with artwork
desperate to speak to Justine.
Family, schools, police service
the greater and lesser states
with pillowcases filled with oranges,
knuckle measurements,
and solitary refinement.
Probes prod the less-than or more-than
for the hinges along the backbone.
The training wheels stay on
so the do-it-yourself kits
won't need to kick in.
The mantras for every sense
don't distract but erase perspective
and focus envy on goods and services.
Any way among the matrix
leads to the dream that runs amuck.

Treasure / Trash

"Make your yard sale signs noticeable! BIG and bright with big letters and big arrows. Make lots of signs including one in front of your house. You can even make a certain symbol that makes your sign unique (such as a star). Place the date and street name on your signs. Use bright fluorescent poster board on top of cardboard for extra strength in case of winds. Check to see if you can read your own signs as you drive by."

Tortoises

We wear articles of clothing
as though they were homes.
Our shirts are kitchens—
our pants, the master bedrooms
with fireplaces and Jacuzzis.
There is plenty of living room.

A father hides beneath a bed,
so he won't lose his pockets.
Spooning couples seek shelter
from the loose ends filling their shoes
and so dig themselves into sheets. Boo.
Alarmed neighbors stretch midriff
material and return to sleep.

Suburban houses, where
each family lies buried in laundry,
are shelved spandex body suits
plumbed for the song, the dance.

Chew, Chew, Chew

The engineer for the gravy train
rides in a bank where the leverages
and throttle function. Bread crumbs
left behind sop up the tracks
that would permit conviction
by a poor slob or taxpayer.

No one in the farming towns
passed through has any beef
after the electricity and internal
combustion impress upon people
going nowhere. The countryside
drools copper and nickel
when payday chugs up the credit line
to blur fat cats for the potato digger.
Even city commuters go hungry
for success on the green line.

New friends and fast runners
cling to the caboose and first
to lose shirts when the vaults
careen off the bridge to heaven
into Rock Bottom Ravine.

Frosting on the cake:
The Antoinette Express
has already left Newburg station.
Brimming with greed,
passengers hold on to vats.

Gullet Gulch

The Grand Canyon between
promise and practice swallows cities
slopping in garbage and plans.
The two lips resist buttoning
or bridge-building.
The landfill that might satiate
with a belly-laugh sits wealthy,
a mountain top with suspension cables.
Guffaws send airwaves across gulps
and burps up broken dreams
and masticated lives.
Yawning signs give "heads up"
on both sides along the road.

Oh, Ouroboros nose!
Students stick to ribs
while blue collar workers
get caught in the craw.
Dead pigs line the riverbed
where pork sandwiches reign.
A nation with diverse engagements
decomposes in bowels at banks.
The unemployed articulation
to the past empties the digestive tract.

Human Resources Department

Mining human resources,
The Cranium and Ligament
Exploitation Corporation saps
consciousness while drilling
for energy. Lights switch on
around the world but short out
enlightenment to dim wit
headlamps, while a double chain
scraper conveyor boom cleans
lifetimes and wallets
for headquarters incorporated.
In the end, the brilliance
for the tunnel boring machine
strips away from the sides
personhood embedded
in psyches, rendering
freedom unnecessary.
The Division for Coercion—
rewards and punishments—
carves holes and right angles
through talents and intellects
day in and day out until
the grateful stick figure flops
beneath a flower bed.

The Log Jam

The loggers in flannel shirts
of red tape, perching themselves
over a loose leaf, roll
each other into a drink,
shuffling their way down
a mountainside into a pickle barrel.
The trees drifting and damming
downstream to a cousin's mill
have not been cut; they are uprooted,
re-routed. Tripped-up filing cabinets
and swivel chairs on their faces
pave a ten lane expressway
that is not traveled again.
In a couple of decades
the agency is bald, battered,
ridden with the threat of dust storms.
Tuning out the river
of computer screens
with fish eyes, the lumbering jack
instinctively knows how to wear wool.
The avalanche of electrical poles
shocks only those who get lost easily.

With Matching Cheers

Interiority designers size the walls
and pace out the floor for patterns
into which organs can't resist
and extremities relax into habit.
The owner pays the price
where the imagination gawks out
the windows or a policeman drops
dead in the living room:
a great deal for mad men with time.

Symmetrical psychologists once delivered
vases in an order, listened to the odds and ends
list this way and, of course, that.
Whole cultures tucked their faith inside bodies
using bold contrasts and pulled shades.
See saw balanced yesterday and today.

Parental stencils sprayed cookie cutter cuties
on walls in small caves. Nooks and crannies
absorbed the graffiti and batter.
Animal crackers ran with the pack
or were lifted from the box.

But every town hall had a cemetery
around it. Store clerks wouldn't wake,
and pedestrians bumped into doors.
The plains and coast made excellent drill teams,
but no flags marked foul territory,
a beginning. The end took care of itself,
in nakedness and with remnant luggage
keeping calm the bay.

When Zen pastors arrived with flat colors,
square meals, and the hope found
in irregular heartbeats, the gastric / intestinal relief
appeared with stoic faces.

How much salt water can lungs hold?

The accidents don't undo themselves with reason.
Pulling closed illusion to hide the freak show,
sleepwalkers shout, "Good morning."

The Church Lot

With representatives who gather
into mobs each morning,
the carnival claims the state well
into the evening. Mad men stop beating wives
and roam the grounds adjusting jaws
and adding jests to summon rides to hospitals.

To distance noses from mole and sledge hammers,
concession stands give out prizes
to anyone playing games with help.
The governors pacing the rides
bypass laws and permit kids with kids
and working stiffs into the dizzy land.

Jokes go round and rough
to expose asses from frowns in merrymaking:
Teenage girls experimenting with the attractions
—soon maids to pull donkeys for goats.

The state police sic hallucinogens
and grass sniffing gods. When heat beats
and cops pop, dads in drool drop.

Ring leaders and their mayors
with arms hidden by cotton candy
and belts holding hops, get caught up
and let loose all change, frisked
from common senses and childhood dreams.

Finally, a city hall's angels arrived
so that every citizen receives some punch,
a hit, a kick, a stab between the ribs.
A local official who wasn't present
told newspapers that shells found at the scene
prove nuts infiltrated the crowd.

A high priest reports that a miracle
has been involved because the money raised
for charities has been saved.

The Law and the Crooked

Atonement festivals twist television
cameras into faces, quarter slums
and trailer parks, but after police
pour light into the alleys and citizens
carve patriotism into county jails,
legend owns the turf and promotes
from within. Dragnets sweep corners
to streets for facts but leave the irrational
and passionate behind. Vigilantes
envision glory and so hear sirens
screeching as lacking enough agony
from culprits. In past centuries,
pikes and the panopticon taught little
where a trio – prosecutor, persecutor,
and prey – each pled for something
different. The gift that keeps on giving,
the fun that creates its own sun echoes
with memory let loose on screens.

City Welfare

The sky is threadbare these mornings.
When the horizons are put on,
the sun is out at the elbows.
Patches of haze, dirtying,
wrinkling the fabric of everything,
tear at hearts, the cowhides till pennies tinkle
down streets to save undeveloped land
of millionaires. When the occupants of the planet are
at their brightest and buildings
are hunching, everyone thanks each other
for their contribution.
Then the civilization exposes itself
to the evening wind, and vagrant shreds
of blue and gold are blown
like kisses around city squares.

The Astrodome

Stars, lowered to the ends of telephone poles
that prop the big top smog,
flag the small dream into reach.

The cab driver stirs in a new car.
The executive wakes to find a trapeze artist
in his arms each morning.

Philosopher and prophet carcasses
are shoveled to the roadside.

Leaning upon evening, shepherds
without homes or love wander hillsides in packs.

Within the constellations
and isolated from the influence of wonder,
technicians bind the bumped foreheads
while a massive birth propels
them all through the barrage of accidents.

Practically Addicted

Free-basing useful knowledge
for suburbia's rolled bill,
the university directs trafficking
between the industrial parks
and single family oblivion.

Addicted to ghettos and dales,
the two nostrils of tree-lined streets
and smiling picket fences inhale
the scholars pilgrimaging to security's
talisman against night and might.

Left to poet's, philosopher's,
and street person's sobriety,
the congested slums paint a healthy sky above
a split level's redundant green.

The border patrol, customs agents,
and vice-squad rake in gadgets
from cities while in pursuit of real estate.
Thoughts that were sent to correction institutes
learn the trade of building homes.

Cables Home

Brooklyn Bridges spanned
from the old world countryside
to ethnic neighborhoods. Who
was kidding whom? Children
traveled over backs that parents
stretched across oceans.
The young invaders were instructed
by Sir Walter Raleigh: "Succeed."
A craft buoyed each generation with a plan.
Give me, give me, give me
has always been the shore lines
and the cry from the river mouths.
While infiltrators fabricated "home,"
language barriers exposed
opportunity for exploitation.
Whoever from the grade school intruders
survived hunger, abuse, molestation
went on to graduate from ivy halls.
Many young alien trespassers dried
upon bleachers to later hunker
down in flats or bungalows with elders.
Sixty years later grandchildren
claim birthright: The best in everything
that the world offers –
"It's mine, it's mine, it's mine."

The Yankee at Home

When cheap mechanical fads fail,
the bona fide bandits first plunder
with plastic imitation the world's artifacts,
hold advertisements from ear to ear,
and then snatch a wallet and head for a house.

Crazed garages gorging and regurgitating
private property, hang over the junkyard,
the summer's blue, red, and white lawn ornaments
flagging flamingo on vacation.

To prove themselves the victims and the heirs
of earth's hula hoop fortune, the bologna
and white bread tuck into back pockets
empty consciences and send the meek on their way.

Gambling with gadgets and anguishing
over objet d'art, the international ingenuity brigade
plucked their play from Pompeii.

The Baggage Claim

We carry our suitcases on our shoulders
while espousing philosophies
on pennant stickers, as though
we each had one that wasn't a corkscrew
for the wine of our urges.

The old communist drank vodka
and thought he wished to travel the world.
He was a suspicious dirt farmer
who didn't even talk to himself;
he kept his will buried in a box.

The water-sipping democrat
infests hotels of cities everywhere
with laundered cash, an ego
the prize of Texas, and a heart that rustles
sour containers in restaurant alleyways.

I see you through the collar of light
where the lid fits the body of the valise.
With gush and flush, we mock
when we meet, our Socratic monologues,
the tabula rasa on which we make our stands.

The Paper Cup World

Dispensed for the splash of spring water
a moment before they are crumpled
by a new generation of clerks,

city walls will be interred
in plastic bags for detonation
by a developer's archaeological instincts.

The stoneware and pewter of forest accountants
carried the art of symmetry to the lips
of today's schoolboy's shortsighted self-esteem:

the enemy at the gates drank bronze and flint.

Cupping mountains and shorelines over a fire,
the hunter was then able to carry his attention
to fields and beg for rain.

Towers of coned and waxed paper
piercing the glassy wet sky
curse paint's blood and are forgotten.

Having no names to memorize and build on,
architects recycle recent ideas and shoot
planned obsolescence into their Grecian urns.

And Every Day Is a Hard Head Day

Waiting for the new knowledge
to sink in, I try to cut it
with animation, but am corked
by know-it-alls accusing me
of thinking I know it all.

Facts, settling like stagnant puddles
seep through the roof.
Leaks are the only way for information
to flood. Every shingle
must be waterlogged
for the people of the body.
And to leave them behind
is to mumble after inventing the chair.

Tomorrow any or all
of the statements could be
stated away for at least the time being,
but sink your investments
upon the next breath.
The atmosphere, the sky,
I send the clouds in
to clarify the peaks of being.

Standard Royal Flush

Each moment we frisk
our pockets for the future
stuffed there decades ago
by scientific salesmen.

The hammock, the backyard
of a craved new world are empty
(as books may as well be) today.
At the last minute
the democratic money
has most of the population green,
the same old few
portraits in the deep black;
the deep red borders slavery.

Now, even, we hawk
our copper pipes for the lousy change
slapped in our reformed palms,
and as if to do plastic surgery,
we fish for specific antiques
to deal with the stacked deck.

Sure, there is the human factor,
the pickpocket, the unexpected
natural phenomenon aging
the slack sleeves,
but the top hat, paraded
in the middle of this evening
by the laboratory animal
was to be owned by no one.

The Empty Busy Time Bomb

The barrels, strategically planted
around your day for wasted time,
dump guilt into the back of your head.

Processed from deep breath's nothingness
and the study of natural sciences,
second hands spur you into the frothing gallop.

A speeding train packing time
with a mile of boxcars heavy with sincere efforts
that bring results, you are unable to stop
for a cow's moo, or slow down if a school bus crosses.

Squeaking through old age, eking into death,
your memory, needing to feed on aged idle hours,
cannot now please its belly, and buries
itself in dream and the garbage
that points the finger at the victim.

The Cameo Crowd

Programmed to fail by parents, schools,
city planners, the communities of learned
helplessness take on the dangerous duty
of war, fast food, and alcohol. With circuits

ripped from their boards by an earlier
generation of family members, the children
of second and third chances burn down
houses from which they cannot escape.

The police departments teach every lesson
learned by the students of sacrifice. Honored
at military funerals, mythologized by fellow
revelers who laughed, pointed fingers,

and went off to college, the chain-smoking
gang huddled outside city hall digs any hole
needing to be dug and stands, the blueprint's
foundation of someone else's urban sprawl.

Now Clones

Suckers for the fantasy bribe
come into the world each moment
and never wean themselves
from their accomplishing
as accomplices their victimhood.
The mug and half-Nelson
flip sides of police records platinum.
Parking lots slurp air
from mall stores that wait
for emergency transfusions
from trailer trucks. The point
above prime scene flashes
naked body parts, its ongoing spectacle,
to make lemonade from threat,
contusion, and a sack of money.
Even uneven accumulation of stealth
by Dow blows its cover at closing bell.
The Jones witness while at work
climbing line graphs and eating charts.
That race leaves its spurs
in the sides of the crime ribs
grilling in custody. Mandatory
sentences one hundred times
won't ground the Yank dreaming
how martyrdom will please him rich.
The other world cuts and trimmings
can't fill its nonsense thieves now either.
Playing dress up parties are contagious
and leave so many petty criminals
in alleys bludgeoned by innocent dictums.
In a fallacy luxury cars and luxury cars away
today poverty and death never happen.

Acknowledgments

Ahadada Books; Anomalous; Black River Review; Blaze Vox; Blood Lotus; Celebration; Confrontation Magazine; Diode; Eoagh; Epiphany Magazine; Eudaimonia; Fact-Simile; Forty Ounce Bachelors; Full Circle Journal; Grand Street; Greenfield Review; Humber Pie; Iconoclast; In Parentheses; Jack Magazine; James Dickey Review; Kansas Quarterly; MediaVirus; Memorious; New Letters; New Writing: An Anthology of Poetry, Fiction, Nonfiction, Drama: The Best of Americana; NOÖ Journal; Orion Headless; Pank Magazine; Paper Tiger; Pemmican; Pennsylvania Review; Pleiades; Poems Niederngasse; Rio: A Journal of Arts; Sangam Literary Magazine; Seems Magazine; Straitjackets; Sulpher River Review; Synaesthetic; Talon Magazine; The Mad-Hatter; Thin Air; War, Literature, and Art: Journal on the Humanities

Thanks to Jared Smith for his good reading as a poet and for his advice.

About the Author

Rich Murphy's credits include two other books: *The Apple in the Monkey Tree* (Codhill Press) and *Voyeur* 2008 Gival Press Poetry Award (Gival Press). He has published six chapbooks: *Great Grandfather* (Pudding House Press), *Family Secret* (Finishing Line Press), *Hunting and Pecking* (Ahadada Books), *Rescue Lines* (Right Hand Pointing), *Phoems for Mobile Vices* (BlazeVox), and *Paideia* (Aldrich Press).

Recent prose scholarship on poetics has been published in *The International Journal of the Humanities, Reconfigurations: A Journal of Poetry and Poetics, The Journal of Ecocriticism*, and *New Writing: The International Journal for the Practice and Theory of Creative Writing*. Rich has taught academic and creative writing at several colleges and universities.

CPSIA information can be obtained at www.ICGtesting.com
Printed in the USA
BVOW03s1529160316

440098BV00004B/7/P